6. Pray for God's help. Y
order to understand what you study in th
would be an appropriate verse for you to

7. *Class teachers using this course for group study will find some helpful suggestions on page 79.*

how to

take the self-check tests

Each lesson is concluded with a test designed to help you evaluate what you have learned.

1. Review the lesson carefully in the light of the self-check test questions.

2. If there are any questions in the self-check test you cannot answer, perhaps you have written into your lesson the wrong answer from your Bible. Go over your work carefully to make sure you have filled in the blanks correctly.

3. When you think you are ready to take the self-check test, do so without looking up the answers.

4. Check your answers to the self-check test carefully with the answer key given on page 80.

5. If you have any questions wrong, your answer key will tell you where to find the correct answers in your lesson. Go back and locate the right answers. Learn by your mistakes!

apply

what you have learned

to your own life

In this connection, read carefully JAMES 1:22-25. It is only as you apply your lessons to your own life that you will really grow in grace and increase in the knowledge of God.

Requisites of Bible Study

Old Testament

1. The Pentateuch—the fivefold "book of the law" (JOSHUA 1:8)

Name these first five books of the Bible. (1) _____

(2) _____ (3) _____ (4) _____

(5) _____

2. Historical books

From the books of the Old Testament listed on the opening pages of your Bible, write the names of the next twelve, and you will have the historical books.

(6) _____ (7) _____ (8) _____

(9) _____ (10) _____ (11) _____

(12) _____ (13) _____ (14) _____

(15) _____ (16) _____ (17) _____

3. Poetical books

These are the next five. (18) _____ (19) _____

(20) _____ (21) _____ (22) _____

4. Prophetical books

These are the last seventeen of the Old Testament.

(23) _____ (24) _____ (25) _____

(26) _____ (27) _____ (28) _____

(29) _____ (30) _____ (31) _____

(32) _____ (33) _____ (34) _____

(35) _____ (36) _____ (37) _____

(38) _____ (39) _____

5. How many books in the Old Testament? _____

New Testament

Note that, according to the following classification, these books are not always in consecutive order.

6. Historical

(1) _____ (2) _____ (3) _____

(4) _____ (5) _____

7. Doctrinal—Christian teaching

(6) _____ (9) _____ (19) _____

8. Church order

(7) _____ (8) _____ (15) _____

(17) _____

9. Church truth

(10) ――――― (12) ―――――

10. Christian life

(11) ――――― (13) ――――― (18) ―――――

(20) ――――― (21) ――――― (23) ―――――

11. Course of this Church age

(14) ――――― (16) ――――― (22) ―――――

(24) ――――― (25) ――――― (26) ―――――

12. Prophetic

The last New Testament book foretells the climax of this Church

age and the Kingdom age. (27) ―――――――――

You will note that there are thirty-nine Old Testament books, twenty-seven in the New Testament, sixty-six in all.

Rightly dividing the Word of Truth

In studying any portion of the Bible it is well to determine the

> Place—where written
> Person—by whom written
> People—to whom principally written
> Purpose—for which written
> Period—at which written

GENESIS 1:1–11:9—Jew and Gentile as a common race. All, as human beings, have a common descent from Adam (ACTS 17:26). GENESIS 11:10–MALACHI 4:6—Israel primarily; the Church veiled (EPHESIANS 3:9, 10); Gentiles mentioned.

The four Gospels—Jews primarily; Church mentioned as about to appear (MATTHEW 28:19, 20).

ACTS 1:1—REVELATION 4:1—Jews temporarily set aside; Gentiles and Jews as individuals, especially Gentiles, become object of God's special favor.

REVELATION 4:1—19:21—Gentiles; Jews regathered; apostate Christendom.

Conditions of fruitful study

The necessity for spiritual sight

13. What class of persons cannot expect to understand Bible truth?

I CORINTHIANS 2:14 _____

One may have the most complete natural faculties of mind, but without the illumination of the Holy Spirit, he cannot perceive spiritual things.

14. How only can we know spiritual things?

I CORINTHIANS 2:9-12 _____

This accounts for foolish statements about Biblical matters from so-called scholarly men who are not regenerated.

15. What should the believer's prayer be as he approaches God's Word?

PSALM 119:18 _____

_____

The Holy Spirit—the true Teacher

16. Who can best teach Bible truth?

Psalm 119:33, 34 _____

The Author knows more about the meaning of His Book than does anyone else. The Bible will never be a dry Book to one who knows its Author.

17. Need any believer depend upon human instruction?

I John 2:27 _____

This does not mean that one can understand everything at once. Leave your difficulties with God until He is pleased to give you better light. "The secret things belong unto the Lord our God: but those things which are revealed belong unto us" (Deuteronomy 29:29).

The Bible—its own interpreter

Spurgeon once said: "The Bible sometimes throws much light upon the commentaries."

18. The Bible is its own best interpreter. Why is the Bible light on Bible difficulties best?

I Corinthians 2:13 _____

Use the marginal references in your Bible. Use your concordance. Use a topical textbook. These are real Bible tools.

You have just studied some important truths about the requisites of Bible study. Review your study by rereading the questions and your written answers. If you wish, you may use the self-check test as an aid in reviewing your lesson. If you aren't sure of an answer, reread the Scripture portion given to see if you can find the answer. Then take this test to see how well you understand important truths you have studied.

In the right-hand margin write "True" or "False" after each of the following statements.

1. The student of the Bible needs the Holy Spirit to illumine the Word of God. _____

2. There are no prophetical books in the New Testament. _____

3. The book of Job is a historical book. _____

4. The natural man can expect to understand Bible truth. _____

5. There are thirty-nine books in the Old Testament. _____

6. The prophetical books of the Old Testament are found at the end of the Old Testament. _____

7. The Bible is its own best interpreter. _____

8. The book of Acts is a prophetical book. _____

9. The first five books in the Bible are called the "books of the law.' _____

10. The total number of historical books in the New Testament is four. _____

Turn to page 80 and check your answers.

Inspiration of the Scriptures

If we cannot believe what the Bible says about itself, we have no logical reason for believing what it says on any subject. Let us examine some of its own claims.

1. Why are the Scripture writings the basis of all morality?

II TIMOTHY 3:16 _____

2. For this reason, what will they do for the believer?

II TIMOTHY 3:17 _____

3. How were the prophets led to write their predictions?

II PETER 1:21 _____

Their yielded mental faculties were "borne along" by the Spirit, so that they wrote what He pleased, whether they understood it or not. Compare I CORINTHIANS 2:13.

4. Did the writers always understand the meaning of the words they wrote?

I PETER 1:10, 11; DANIEL 12:8, 9 _____

5. What was the divine purpose in giving these messages?

ROMANS 15:4; I CORINTHIANS 10:11 _____

Christ's testimony to the Old Testament

6. What did Jesus say about the three Jewish divisions of the Old Testament?

LUKE 24:44 _____

_____

7. How did Jesus state the great purpose of the Old Testament?

JOHN 5:39 _____

8. What did Jesus call the Old Testament?

MARK 7:13 _____

9. What strong assertion did Jesus make?

MATTHEW 5:18; 24:35 _____

_____

10. Is it possible to believe in the Lord Jesus without accepting these Old Testament writings?

JOHN 5:46, 47 _____

Christ's testimony to the New Testament

11. What did Jesus say His disciples should do?

JOHN 15:27 _____

12. Would they be left dependent upon their own recollections?

JOHN 14:26 _____

13. Were there some truths to be revealed to them which Jesus Himself did not give?

JOHN 16:12 _____

14. How would the divine revelation be completed?

JOHN 16:13 _____

15. What authority did Jesus give to their words?

LUKE 10:16 _____

16. Through whose words, would men be saved after Jesus left the world?

JOHN 17:20 _____

It is evident that no one can profess to be a follower of the Lord Jesus without accepting the entire Bible.

In what sense is the Bible inspired?

The word "inspiration" in II TIMOTHY 3:16 means "God-breathed" or "filled with the breath of God." (See PSALM 33:6.) It means the breathing of God by the Holy Spirit into men, qualifying them to receive and record divine truth.

17. What could any inspired writer say?

II SAMUEL 23:2 _____

_____

18. What did Jeremiah claim?

JEREMIAH 1:9 _____

_____

19. What did Ezekiel claim?

EZEKIEL 2:2 _____

_____

20. What did Hosea claim?

HOSEA 1:1 _____

_____

21. What did Joel claim to have received?

JOEL 1:1 _____

_____

22. What did Amos claim to give forth?

AMOS 7:14-16 _____

_____

23. Where did Paul receive his wisdom in spiritual things?

I CORINTHIANS 2:13 _____

The expressions, "Thus saith the LORD," and "God said," occur hundreds of times in the Bible. No other book makes such claims; nor is any writer since Bible times inspired in the same sense.

Divine inspiration is not:

a. Poetic ecstacy. This theory of inspiration is the working basis of rationalism.

b. Mental illumination. A consecrated believer may receive spiritual light for the understanding of divine truth, but this does not approach the inspiration described in the Bible.

c. Inspired concepts. Some say there are "inspired thoughts" in the Bible, but the writers often blundered in trying to express these thoughts. This is contrary to Scripture.

d. Verbal dictation. The writers were not mere machines or stenographers taking dictation.

Divine inspiration is:

The work of the Holy Spirit. He so controlled the writers that the language they used conveyed the divine meaning and did not pervert it. This did not destroy the writers' individuality or personal style. We have God's Word in their style.

check-up time No. 2

You have just studied some important truths about the inspiration of the Scriptures. Review your study by rereading the questions and your written answers. If you aren't sure of an answer, reread the Scripture portion given to see if you can find the answer. Then take the following test to see how well you understand important truths you have studied.

In the right-hand margin write "True" or "False" after each of the following statements.

1. It is possible to believe in Christ without accepting the Old Testament writings as the Word of God. _____

2. The writers of Scripture depended entirely upon their own knowledge for the writng of their books. _____

3. One of the purposes of the Old Testament was to reveal Christ. _____

4. The writers of Scripture understood all that they wrote. _____

5. The Holy Spirit was promised by Christ to the disciples to complete the revelation concerning Christ. _____

6. Experiences in the lives of Old Testament individuals are recorded as examples for the instruction of the reader today. _____

7. Jesus called the Old Testament "the word of God." _____

8. The Word of God will abide longer than the heaven and the earth. _____

9. No Old Testament writer claimed that his message had come directly from God. _____

10. Jesus recognized as Scripture the Jewish divisions of the Old Testament. _____

Turn to page 80 and check your answers.

Bible Doctrine of God

Why believe in a personal God?

1. How are His eternal power and Godhead made known?

ROMANS 1:20 _____

2. What testimony to His existence goes forth daily to all the earth?

PSALM 19:1-4 _____

_____

3. What argument must be drawn from marks of design?

HEBREWS 3:4 _____

4. What does faith invariably teach?

HEBREWS 11:3 _____

_____

5. Every effect has a cause. The universe is an effect and must owe its existence to a Cause fully equal to its production. What kind of Cause would such effects call for?

_____

6. A system of order is evident in the universe. Things work harmoniously together toward certain ends. This must have been designed. What must be inferred as to the intellect of such a Designer?

_____

7. The personality and moral nature of man cannot be accounted for merely on the ground of material and unconscious forces. Man possesses reason, conscience, will. What does this presuppose as to the Source from whom such a being as man must have come?

_____

Man's instinctive idea of a true God

8. Another strong argument for belief in a personal God is inferred from the very ideas found in the human mind. Millions have a notion of an infinite and perfect God. This very idea involves a higher degree of reality than belongs to man. How was this instinctive idea stamped upon the human mind? Who must have been its Author?

God's revelation of Himself

9. Since there is a God, surely He has found some way to reveal truth concerning Himself to intelligent creatures made by Him. In what two ways has this revelation been made?

HEBREWS 1:1, 2 _____

10. Rationalists are endeavoring to make "God" and "the world" identical in meaning. They say the law of the universe is God, that He is not distinct from the universe, but a part of it—the force which has developed the world through a process of evolution. But let us take the testimony of His own revelation, the authenticity of which is discussed in another lesson. Is God distinguished from all the works of His hands?

JEREMIAH 10:10-16; ACTS 14:15 _____

11. Is He personally, actively present in the affairs of the universe?

PSALM 104:27-34; MATTHEW 6:26-30; 10:29-34 _____

Personality does not necessarily involve a physical body. It is characterized by knowledge, feeling, will.

14

12. What is said as to God's visibility?

JOHN 1:18; I TIMOTHY 1:17; 6:16 _____

_____

13. According to Scripture, is it not correct to say that God is incorporeal, invisible reality?

JOHN 4:24; ACTS 17:24, 25 _____

_____

_____

14. Is God limited by any bounds of time?

PSALM 90:2, 4 _____

15. What is said of the unchangeableness of His character and purpose?

JAMES 1:17 _____

_____

16. Is He dependent in any way for His existence?

JOHN 5:26 _____

17. What is said of His omnipresence?

JEREMIAH 23:23, 24 _____

_____

18. How extensive are His powers?

MATTHEW 19:26 _____

_____

19. Are there any limits to His knowledge?

PSALM 147:5; I JOHN 3:20 _____

_____

The Holy Trinity

20. How does the Scripture answer the notion that there may be many gods—idols made by the hands of men?

a. DEUTERONOMY 4:35 _____

b. ISAIAH 44:6 _____

c. I TIMOTHY 2:5 _____

The unity of the Godhead is a truth fundamental to the doctrine of the Trinity, not a contradiction of it.

21. There is one God, but the Godhead (ROMANS 1:20; COLOSSIANS 2:9) subsists in a personality which is threefold. Accordingly, how is God made known to man?

MATTHEW 28:19 _____

Notice that the word "name," in this verse is in the singular. "Father . . . Son . . . and Holy Ghost" is the final name of the one true God. ("Holy Ghost" is the old English translation of "Holy Spirit.")

22. How does the Old Testament show this plurality in the one Godhead?

a. GENESIS 1:26 _____

_____

b. GENESIS 11:6, 7 _____

c. ISAIAH 6:8 _____

23. How is this Trinity in unity seen in the following verses?

a. JOHN 14:16 _____

_____

b. MARK 1:10, 11 _____

_____

c. EPHESIANS 2:18 _____

_____

The Bible further witnesses to the Trinity in the Godhead by ascribing deity and the attributes of God, both to Jesus Christ and to the Holy Spirit.

24. How does God refer to His Son in the following verses?

a. HEBREWS 1:8 _____

b. I CORINTHIANS 15:47 _____

c. PHILIPPIANS 2:6 _____

25. What claim did Jesus Himself make as to His divine origin and powers?

a. JOHN 5:17-23 _____

_____

b. MATTHEW 28:18 _____

c. JOHN 14:7-10 _____

_____

26. How is omnipotence ascribed to Jesus?

HEBREWS 1:3 _____

27. How is omniscience ascribed to Him?

COLOSSIANS 2:3 _____

28. What part did Jesus have in creation?

a. JOHN 1:3 _____

b. COLOSSIANS 1:16 _____

_____

c. HEBREWS 1:2, 3 _____

29. How is He described?

a. JOHN 1:14 _____

_____

b. I TIMOTHY 3:16 _____

_____

30. What is the meaning of His name, "Immanuel"?

ISAIAH 7:14; MATTHEW 1:23 _____

31. What are all angels and every other creature commanded to do?

a. HEBREWS 1:6 _____

b. PHILIPPIANS 2:10, 11 _____

_____

32. In Christ dwells all the fullness of whom?

COLOSSIANS 2:9; 1:19 _____

33. What position has He?

COLOSSIANS 2:10; EPHESIANS 1:21 _____

34. Do such references leave any room for doubt that Jesus is One of the Godhead?

_____

You will also find that powers belonging only to God are ascribed to the Holy Spiirt. For example, see HEBREWS 9:14; PSALM 139:7-10; LUKE 1:35; I CORINTHIANS 2:10, 11; JOHN 16:12, 13; 14:26; PSALM 104:30; JOHN 6:63; II PETER 1:21; ACTS 5:3, 4.

35. Do such references leave any room for doubt that the Holy Spirit is One of the Godhead?

_____

check-up time No. 3

You have just studied some important truths about the Bible doctrine of God. Review your study by re-reading the questions and your written answers. If you aren't sure of an answer, reread the Scripture portion given to see if you can find the answer. Then take this test to see how well you understand important truths you have studied.

In the right-hand margin write "True" or "False" after each of the following statements.

1. The Godhead exists in a threefold personality. _____

2. God is present everywhere. _____

3. In the Scriptures the Lord Jesus is described as above all creation. _____

4. Creation is a witness to God's existence. _____

5. Omnipotence is ascribed to Jesus in the Scriptures. _____

6. There is no limit to the power of God. _____

7. Christ had a part in creation. _____

8. "God" and "the world" are identical in meaning. _____

9. Deity is ascribed to the Holy Spirit in the Scriptures. _____

10. Jesus claimed to be equal with God the Father. _____

Turn to page 80 and check your answers.

Bible Teaching About Christ's Pre-existence and Incarnation

His pre-existence

Unbelief has changed its emphasis in recent years. There are religious leaders who acknowledge the so-called "divinity" of Christ, but their explanation is that God is in human nature and that all are sons of God, even as Jesus was.

1. What does the Bible say? What did the Lord Jesus say of Himself?

LUKE 10:22 _____

_____

2. Is any human being a son of God in the sense in which Jesus possesses Sonship?

I JOHN 5:10-12 _____

_____

3. Can anyone know God without acknowledging the unique Sonship of Christ?

I JOHN 2:23 _____

4. What gives to the love of God its unparalleled glory?

I JOHN 4:9, 10 _____

_____

5. What do we read in John 1:1-3 about the eternity of Jesus Christ?

_____

_____

6. What did Jesus say of His pre-existence?

John 8:58 _____

7. What did the prophet say of the pre-existence of the coming Saviour?

Micah 5:2 _____

_____

Compare what is said of God the Father in Psalm 90:2.

8. Did Jesus become Son of God in His incarnation, or was He God's Son prior to that?

Galatians 4:4 _____

9. How does this compare with what Jesus said of Himself?

John 16:27, 28; 6:38, 62 _____

_____

10. How far back does His pre-existence go?

Colossians 1:17 _____

11. How did Jesus express His pre-existence in His great intercessory prayer?

John 17:5, 24 _____

_____

12. In what does the marvelous grace of Jesus Christ consist?

II Corinthians 8:9 _____

_____

21

Read PROVERBS 8:22-36, remembering that here Wisdom is personified and speaks of Christ. Compare COLOSSIANS 2:3; I CORINTHIANS 1:24.

13. How has God "the Father . . . delivered us from the power of darkness, and . . . translated us into the kingdom of his dear Son"?

COLOSSIANS 1:14; compare 1:12-16, 18 _____

_____

His incarnation

We have seen that Jesus Christ was pre-existent. His virgin birth was a step in God's redemptive plan (GALATIANS 4:4).

14. Centuries before the birth of Christ, what "sign" did the prophet say God would give, by which the Saviour of the world could be positively identified?

ISAIAH 7:14 _____

_____

15. Has the world ever known of any other virgin birth or absolutely holy conception?

_____

16. Why can no one ever be compared with the Lord Jesus?

_____

17. What were the circumstances surrounding the birth of Jesus?

MATTHEW 1:22, 23 _____

_____

_____

This should have been accepted as the unmistakable sign to lost humanity that God had come to redeem and lift men up to Himself.

18. Was it so accepted?

JOHN 1:11 _____

19. Why not?

JOHN 3:19 _____

_____

20. Of whose Person was Jesus the "express image"?

HEBREWS 1:3 _____

21. What expressions indicate that the eternal Son entered this world through this human gateway, by His own will?

HEBREWS 2:14, 16 _____

_____

22. He who was eternal God "took upon him the form of" whom?

PHILIPPIANS 2:6, 7 _____

He did not lay aside His deity, but voluntarily laid aside His glory. Remember that it was only His human nature that was born of Mary.

23. Is it any wonder that angelic forces burst into praise over such a stupendous event?

LUKE 2:13, 14 _____

His purpose in His incarnation

24. What was Christ's supreme purpose in coming to earth?

a. GALATIANS 4:4, 5 _____

b. PHILIPPIANS 2:8 _____

25. Why was He, for the time, made lower than the angels?

HEBREWS 2:9 _____

26. Why could He be a sinless, perfect Substitute?

LUKE 1:35 _____

27. How is this perfect holiness accounted for?

MATTHEW 1:20 _____

Here is one Man Satan could search through and through, yet find Him absolutely sinless. He would not respond at any point to satanic suggestion. See, for example, JOHN 8:29, 46; II CORINTHIANS 5:21; HEBREWS 4:15; 7:26; I PETER 2:22; I JOHN 3:5.

28. What is another reason His sacrifice could be accepted for all men?

PHILIPPIANS 2:6, 8 _____

Christ was—and ever shall be—the Lord of glory. His death on Calvary was the most stupendous sacrifice for sin possible.

Conclusion: Christ is "God . . . manifest in the flesh" (I TIMOTHY 3:16)

29. What is the truth about the Person of Jesus?

JOHN 1:14 _____

30. If Jesus was not conceived of the Holy Spirit, could He save anyone from sin?

MATTHEW 1:21 _____

31. If He was not God incarnate, as He Himself claimed (JOHN 5:23-27), what must He have been?

JOHN 7:12 _____

32. If He was not divinely conceived, but born as other men, would it be right to worship Him?

MATTHEW 4:10; 14:33; 28:9; LUKE 24:52. Compare ACTS 10:25,

26; REVELATION 22:8, 9 _____

33. If He was not God incarnate, would He be in a position to save a single soul?

JOHN 3:6; HEBREWS 7:26 _____

You have just studied some important truths about the pre-existence and incarnation of the Lord Jesus Christ. Review your study by rereading the questions and your written answers. If you aren't sure of an answer, reread the Scripture portion given to see if you can find the answer. Then take this test to see how well you understand important truths you have studied.

In the right-hand margin write "True" or "False" after each of the following statements.

1. All human beings are sons of God in the same sense that Jesus possesses Sonship. _____

2. Jesus was the Son of God before His incarnation. _____

3. The Old Testament taught that the Saviour would be born of a virgin. _____

4. Because Christ is God incarnate, He is able to save us. _____

5. It is possible to know God without acknowledging the unique Sonship of Christ. _____

6. The purpose of the incarnation of Christ was to provide redemption for mankind. _____

7. Christ laid aside His deity at the time of His incarnation. _____

8. Christ was sinless. _____

9. Christ taught that He existed before the time of the incarnation, and that He had come from the Father. _____

10. Christ was the "express image" of God. _____

Turn to page 80 and check your answers.

Bible Teaching About Christ's Humanity and Atoning Death

His humanity

Heresies start in misconceptions of the Person and work of Jesus Christ.

1. What warning does Scripture give concerning wrong conceptions of the humanity of Jesus?

I JOHN 4:2, 3 _____

_____

2. Why was it essential that the Son of God should become a human being?

HEBREWS 2:17, 18 _____

_____

_____

3. Read the prophecy of ISAIAH 9:6 carefully. As a Child, Jesus

was _____. As the Son, He was _____.

4. Read JOHN 1:14. As the eternal Word, He "was made" (or,

"became") _____. God could not approach men except in the form of man. He was One of the Godhead, while at the same time He was in the form of man.

5. What did Paul say about the Saviour?

COLOSSIANS 2:9 _____

In the New Testament Jesus is called "Son of man" seventy-seven times. In speaking of Himself He usually took this title. It emphasized the fact that, as the "last Adam," He was the Head of the human race; and it suggested His connection with other men.

As proof of His true humanity, notice the following:

6. As a Child, He _____

_____. LUKE 2:52

7. As a Man, He experienced:

a. _____. MATTHEW 21:18

b. _____. JOHN 19:28

c. _____. JOHN 4:6

d. _____. MATTHEW 8:24

e. _____. HEBREWS 4:15

8. How shall we explain these human limitations in the light of Christ's deity?

PHILIPPIANS 2:7, 8 _____

_____

_____

He could exercise His divine attributes at any time, but He never did so, insofar as it could affect His trial as Man. Never did He use these powers for His own relief.

Some are confused about the humanity of Jesus because they associate the thought with the carnal nature of man. Humanity need not be thought of in terms of man's present condition. Human nature and carnal nature are not the same. The carnal, or sinful, nature has become part of human nature through sin. Jesus did not have a carnal nature because He was conceived of the Holy Spirit, and He never yielded to sin.

9. He was truly human, but in one respect differed from all

men born of women _____. HEBREWS 4:15

10. This involves a great mystery; for sorrow, suffering and death were originally connected with sin. Jesus was a Man of

_____. ISAIAH 53:3

11. The sinless One suffered and died as no other. Whose griefs, sorrows and sins caused His suffering and death?

a. ISAIAH 53:4, 6 _____

b. I CORINTHIANS 15:3 _____

It is not easy for the human mind to reconcile the true humanity and true deity of Jesus. The Bible does not reconcile them, but leaves them as a mystery which we are called upon to believe. Notice how these two truths are placed side by side without explanation.

12. In MATTHEW 8:24-26 what human limitation is seen?

_____

13. What display of divine omnipotence is manifested in MATTHEW 8:26?

_____

14. In JOHN 11:35 what human trait is seen in the Lord Jesus?

_____

15. What divine power did He display in JOHN 11:43, 44?

_____

16. In LUKE 6:12 what human experience did He have?

_____

17. In MATTHEW 16:21 how did He show human submission?

_____

18. How is His humanity declared in HEBREWS 2:14?

_____

19. What is said of Him in HEBREWS 1:3?

_____

20. Jesus was Man, not just for the time of His short sojourn on earth. How did He demonstrate that He was still Man in the resurrection?

a. _____

_____. Luke 24:39

b. _____

_____. John 20:27

21. By what title did Stephen refer to Him when he saw Him in the heavens?

Acts 7:55, 56 _____

22. As our High Priest in heaven, does He still have the form of man?

I Timothy 2:5 _____

23. By what title is He referred to in connection with His second coming?

Matthew 19:28 _____

Because Jesus "suffered being tempted, he is able to succour them that are tempted" (Hebrews 2:18). If He were only Man and not God, He would be as powerless as other men to give us aid. We need human sympathy and understanding, and we must have divine help!

The deeper our sense of His true glory, as God, the deeper will be our faith in Him (Matthew 28:18). The deeper our apprehension of His humbling Himself, as Man, the greater will be our love for Him (Philippians 2:8, 9).

His atoning death

Religions are many; yet there are really but two—God's and man's. Man's religions, of whatever name, are always built on the foundation of self-righteousness. God's religion, revealed in the Bible, rests upon the foundation of the atoning sacrifice of the Lamb of God.

24. How is this distinction asserted in TITUS 3:5, 6?

_____

_____

25. What was the answer of Jesus to the question, "What shall we do" to earn salvation?

JOHN 6:28, 29 _____

_____

_____

"By grace are ye saved through faith . . ." (EPHESIANS 2:8, 9). Good works, in order to be accepted in God's sight, must be the fruit, not the means, of salvation (EPHESIANS 2:10).

26. What does God expect of one who has trusted the Lord Jesus for salvation?

TITUS 3:8 _____

_____

27. What does God say of human righteousness at its best?

ISAIAH 64:6 _____

28. Who alone can supply us with an acceptable garment of salvation?

ISAIAH 61:10 _____

29. How is this righteousness provided for us?

II CORINTHIANS 5:21 _____

_____

30. How can it be obtained?

ROMANS 3:21, 22 _____

_____

31. What gives us boldness to enter into the presence of God?

HEBREWS 10:19, 20 _____

32. What is the one teaching of the Old Testament as pictured in the sacrifices?

LEVITICUS 17:11 _____

_____

33. Why were these blood sacrifices offered by the priests?

HEBREWS 9:6, 7 _____

_____

34. To whose work did they point?

ISAIAH 53:5; JOHN 1:29; HEBREWS 9:9-14 _____

_____

The entire Old Testament system of sacrifices taught that man could do nothing to save himself. He had to accept God's grace by faith. The sinner was pointed to the coming Redeemer, who once for all would offer Himself as the Lamb of God.

35. What was pictured by the perfect lamb of the flock, offered in sacrifice?

EXODUS 12:5; compare I PETER 1:19 _____

_____

As we read the New Testament, we are impressed with the fact that the most prominent truth is that of the death of Christ. It is referred to more than 175 times. His death was the very object of His incarnation—the main purpose for His coming into the world.

36. How did the Lord Himself declare His purpose in coming into the world?

MATTHEW 18:11 _____

_____

37. How was this to be accomplished?

MATTHEW 20:28; 26:28 _____

_____

38. What did God lay upon Jesus as He, the sinless One, hung upon the cross?

ISAIAH 53:6 _____

_____

39. What is the result of a sinner's acceptance of Him?

ROMANS 4:5 _____

40. God accepts no religious creed that ignores the necessity of the blood atonement. Why?

HEBREWS 9:22 _____

_____

41. What is the basis of cleansing from sin?

I JOHN 1:7 _____

42. What was the redemption price?

I PETER 1:19; EPHESIANS 1:7 _____

43. In God's sight, what removes the stain of our sins?

REVELATION 1:5, 6 _____

_____

44. What brings peace to the sinner?

COLOSSIANS 1:20 _____

45. How is the sinner justified before God?

Romans 5:9 _____

46. How are sinners brought nigh to God?

Ephesians 2:13 _____

47. What is the one means of purging a conscience from the sense of sin?

Hebrews 9:14 _____

48. What did the Lord Jesus declare to be the absolute necessity?

Matthew 16:21; John 3:14, 15 _____

49. What will be the theme of the song of the redeemed in heaven?

Revelation 5:6-12; 7:10 _____

_____

_____

Note carefully that Jesus did not die as a martyr or because He was a victim of circumstances.

50. When He foretold His approaching death, what did He also foretell?

Matthew 16:21 _____

_____

51. This proves that _____

_____. John 10:17, 18

Christ died as a ransom for sinners. He died of His own choice and in fulfillment of Old Testament prophecy.

check-up time No. 5

You have just studied some important truths about Christ's humanity and His atoning death. Review your study by rereading the questions and your written answers. If you aren't sure of an answer, reread the Scripture portion given to see if you can find the answer. Then take this test to see how well you understand important truths you have studied.

In the right-hand margin write "True" or "False" after each of the following statements.

1. The only basis of cleansing from sin is the blood of Christ.

2. Man's own righteousness is acceptable to God.

3. Jesus declared that His purpose for coming into the world was to save sinners.

4. The sacrifices of the Old Testament looked forward to the redemptive work of Christ.

5. There is no proof that Christ had a truly human body.

6. In Christ dwells all the fullness of the Godhead bodily.

7. Christ died by accident, as a martyr.

8. The humanity of Christ is seen in the fact that He was hungry at times.

9. The righteousness which man needs is provided only by God through faith in Christ Jesus.

10. In raising the dead, Christ displayed His divine power.

Turn to page 80 and check your answers.

Bible Teaching About Christ's Resurrection

"The Son of man must . . . be raised the third day" (LUKE 9:22). Thus the Lord Jesus foretold the necessity of His bodily resurrection—

To fulfill Old Testament prophecy

1. What prophecy made to the fathers was fulfilled in the resurrection of Jesus?

Read ACTS 2:25-31; 13:32-37.

ACTS 2:27; 13:35 _____

_____

2. How did Christ's resurrection fulfill a prophecy made by Jesus Himself at the beginning of His earthly career?

JOHN 2:19-22 _____

_____

3. What did the Lord Jesus point out after His resurrection?

LUKE 24:45, 46 _____

_____

To put away sin

4. What is true if Christ did not rise from the dead?

I Corinthians 15:17 _____

_____

5. What fully demonstrated His claim to be the Son of God with power?

Romans 1:4 _____

_____

To justify the sinner

6. What was one great purpose of Christ's resurrection?

Romans 4:25 _____

7. What has His resurrection furnished the believer?

Romans 8:34 _____

To inspire faith in the believer

8. If Christ is not risen, what is the result?

I Corinthians 15:14 _____

To assure the believer of a resurrection body

9. What assurance does Christ's resurrection give?

I Corinthians 15:20-23 _____

10. What change will take place in the believer when Christ comes?

I John 3:2 _____

_____

11. What does every believer now confidently await?

ROMANS 8:23 _____

To enable the believer to bear fruit unto God

12. What should be the normal result of being united by the Holy Spirit to the risen Christ?

ROMANS 7:4 _____

_____

To establish Jesus' right to be the Judge of all mankind

13. How has God placed His seal upon Jesus as Judge?

ACTS 17:31 _____ .

Christ's resurrection—an established fact of history

The evidence of Christ's resurrection is established in history beyond any reasonable doubt. The wonder of it is akin to the wonder of His marvelous life and teaching and the majesty of His death.

He was crucified by competent executioners who took no chances.

14. How did they make sure that He was dead?

JOHN 19:34 _____

15. Before giving permisison for the removal of the Lord's body, what did Pilate require?

MARK 15:43-45 _____

_____

When Jesus' resurrection was published abroad, no one suggested that the soldiers had failed to kill Him. There was no question then as to the reality of His death.

16. What did the rulers of the Jews bribe the guards to say?

MATTHEW 28:11-15 _____

17. What chance would the disciples have had to steal the body?

MATTHEW 27:62-66 _____

The hopeless despair on the part of all Christ's followers proves that there was no question as to the reality of His death (JOHN 21:2, 3; LUKE 24:18-21).

18. What act definitely proves that Jesus was really dead?

JOHN 19:39, 40 _____

19. When Mary Magdalene discovered that the tomb of Jesus was empty, what did she think had happened?

JOHN 20:1, 2 _____

20. What did Peter and John find when they reached the tomb?

JOHN 20:3-7 _____

21. What shock did the guards receive?

MATTHEW 28:2-4 _____

22. What was the angel's message to the women?

MATTHEW 28:5, 6 _____

_____

23. Who saw Jesus first?

JOHN 20:11-17 _____

24. Who was favored by a special visit of the risen Saviour?

LUKE 24:34; I CORINTHIANS 15:5 _____

25. To whom did He next appear?

LUKE 24:13-35 _____

26. What was His next appearance?

JOHN 20:19-24 _____

27. To whom did He appear eight days later?

JOHN 20:25, 26 _____

28. Where was His next appearance?

JOHN 21:1-23 _____

29. How many believers saw Him later on a mountain?

I CORINTHIANS 15:6 _____

30. According to I CORINTHIANS 15:7, who saw Him?

_____

31. When did the eleven have their final glimpse of Him?

LUKE 24:50-53; MARK 16:19, 20; ACTS 1:9-12 _____

_____

32. Who were later granted a sight of the glorified Christ?

a. I CORINTHIANS 15:8 _____

b. ACTS 7:55, 56 _____

c. REVELATION 1:9-18 _____

The testimony to the resurrection is twofold: (a) documentary testimony to the facts by witnesses; (b) historic testimony to its consequences and influence upon men.

check-up time No. 6

You have just studied some important truths about Christ's resurrection. Review your study by rereading the questions and your written answers. If you aren't sure of an answer, reread the Scripture portion given to see if you can find the answer. Then take this test to see how well you understand important truths you have studied.

In the right-hand margin write "True" or "False" after each of the following statements.

1. Christ predicted that He would rise from the dead. _____

2. The angel at the tomb announced that Christ was dead. _____

3. The resurrection of Christ was God's seal upon Him as Judge. _____

4. The resurrection of Christ was a demonstration of His deity. _____

5. Because of the resurrection, the believer now has an Intercessor. _____

6. After His resurrection, Christ appeared to five hundred believers at one time. _____

7. The body of the Lord was stolen from the tomb by the disciples. _____

8. If Christ was not raised from the dead, our faith is vain. _____

9. One purpose of Christ's resurrection was to bring justification to all who would believe in Him. _____

10. The first person to see the risen Christ was Nicodemus. _____

Turn to page 80 and check your answers.

Bible Teaching About Christ's Ascension and High Priestly Work

Christ—our Prophet, Priest and King

The Hebrews always ascribed to their coming Messiah a three-fold office. He was to be Prophet, Priest and King. As Prophet, Jesus appeared first as "a teacher come from God" (JOHN 3:2) and "taught . . . as one having authority"—as "never man spake" (MATTHEW 7:29; JOHN 7:46). In His death and ascension, He assumed the function of High Priest. As King, He will return in glory to reign.

His work as Priest is twofold:

1. What did He offer as eternal High Priest?

HEBREWS 10:12 _____

2. What further function of the Priest does He forever fulfill?

HEBREWS 7:25 _____

3. Of what prophecy is this a fulfillment?

ISAIAH 53:12 _____

The seventeenth chapter of John is a wonderful illustration of Christ's intercessory prayer for the saints.

4. When will Jesus fulfill the third feature of Messiah's work?

MATTHEW 25:31-34 _____

As Prophet, Jesus represented God to man. As Priest, He represents believers before God. As King, He will rule for God over all men. We need to know Him in all the fullness of His work: as Prophet, giving us the words of eternal wisdom (COLOSsians 3:16); as Priest who offered a ransom to God for us and who now intercedes for us; as King who now rules over us in a spiritual realm and will come again as promised (Acts 1:11).

His ascension into heaven

5. What was the last promise of the risen Saviour to His disciples?

Luke 24:49; Acts 1:8 _____

6. Having given this promise, what did He do?

Luke 24:50 _____

7. As He spoke, what happened?

Luke 24:51; Acts 1:9 _____

Remember that our Lord's last attitude as He ascended was that of blessing His followers. This is a perpetual sign. Remember also His promise, "Lo, I am with you alway . . ." (Matthew 28:20). It is a declaration of His ability to give the only true happiness and the only power for enduring service.

8. With what feeling did the disciples return to Jerusalem?

Luke 24:52 _____

His work as High Priest

9. Upon entering the heaven of heavens, what did Jesus do?

Mark 16:19 _____

What rejoicing there must have been in heaven when He entered and assumed His place as eternal High Priest! He was now the first of a new race—the last Adam—and He could enter heaven as a Man by the right of His own perfect humanity. He needed no mediator—no mercy was required. He was the first sinless Man to enter there, and heaven was made bright with a beauty and glory unknown to it before.

10. What position of nearness to God does this give to every true believer?

COLOSSIANS 3:1 _____

_____

11. What will this mean when Jesus appears in His second advent?

COLOSSIANS 3:4 _____

_____

Moral distances may be great, but there is no distance between a true child of God and our risen Christ. After His ascension He showed Himself to Stephen; He crossed the path of Saul; He talked to John.

12. As Priest, Christ is "a _____

_____." ROMANS 3:25

Literally, "a propitiatory [sacrifice] . . ."; compare I JOHN 2:2; 4:10.

13. Since believers still have the old nature with its tendency to sin, of what do we all stand in need?

I JOHN 2:1 _____

14. What is one reason the advocacy of Christ for His own cannot fail?

I JOHN 2:1 _____

15. What, therefore, is needed to restore the sinning one to fellowship?

I JOHN 1:9 _____

Thus we see how essential it is that, as believers, we should have a living, interceding High Priest. Even though His death on the cross paid our penalty in full, we need the indwelling Holy Spirit to enable us to live as Christians.

16. Not only are we saved by grace, but we _____

_____. ROMANS 5:2

17. How has God provided resurrection power for our lives here and now? Compare PHILIPPIANS 3:10; EPHESIANS 1:19, 20;

COLOSSIANS 1:27 _____

_____

God foresaw our need of the risen Lord's ministry. Therefore, having finished His atoning work on the cross (JOHN 19:30), Christ "sat down on the right hand of God" (HEBREWS 10:12).

18. Did the priests of old sit down at their work?

HEBREWS 10:11 _____

The work of the priests in Israel was never done. It pointed on to Christ! His finished work tells us that the foundation of our salvation is absolutely complete and can never be repeated. This is the answer to Romanism.

19. The fact that Christ sits "on the right hand of God" also suggests that we may at all times look unto Him as the

_____. HEBREWS 12:2

20. Seeing that we have such a High Priest, what should we do?

HEBREWS 4:14 _____

21. What reason have we to come boldly to Him in prayer?

HEBREWS 4:15, 16 _____

22. What help comes to us in praying, because we have an Intercessor at the throne of grace?

ROMANS 8:26, 27 _____

23. Of what is Jesus' position at the right hand of power also a guarantee?

MARK 14:62; ACTS 1:11 _____

You have just studied some important truths about Christ's ascension and High Priestly work. Review your study by rereading the questions and your written answers. If you aren't sure of an answer, reread the Scripture portion given to see if you can find the answer. Then take this test to see how well you understand important truths you have studied.

In the right-hand margin write "True" or "False" after each of the following statements.

1. Christ can qualify as our Intercessor because He was tempted as we are, but was without sin. _____

2. He will fulfill His office as King when He returns. _____

3. Christ intercedes for the believer today. _____

4. The high priests of the Old Testament sat down after they had finished their work. _____

5. The ascension of Christ to the right hand of power gives assurance of His second coming. _____

6. Christ offered one sacrifice forever for the sins of the people. _____

7. After His ascension, Christ sat down at the right hand of the Father. _____

8. Christ can qualify as the believer's Advocate because He is righteous. _____

9. The disciples were sorry when Christ ascended to heaven. _____

10. Christ is presently the believer's Advocate with the Father. _____

Turn to page 80 and check your answers.

Bible Teaching About Christ's Second Advent

In the Old Testament the greatest number of predictions have to do with Christ's personal, visible advent to reign. In the New Testament His second coming is referred to 318 times; and with its 260 chapters, this means that it is mentioned once in every twenty-five verses.

1. How did Christ come into the world the first time?

a. Born of _____. GALATIANS 4:4

b. Conceived of _____. MATTHEW 1:18-25

2. The Word became _____. JOHN 1:14

3. What did He say about His going away?

a. JOHN 7:33 _____

b. JOHN 17:5 _____

4. For what purpose did He say He was returning to heaven?

JOHN 14:2 _____

5. What promise did He make?

JOHN 14:3 _____

6. Is there a sense in which Jesus is spiritually present with believers while physically absent from the world?

JOHN 14:16, 17; 15:26; 16:7, 14; MATTHEW 28:20; GALATIANS 2:20

_____

7. As to His physical Person, where is Jesus now?

JOHN 17:24; HEBREWS 12:2 _____

The "blessed hope" of the Church

8. While acknowledging His spiritual presence, what is the "blessed hope" of enlightened believers?

_____

_____

See, for example, Titus 2:13; Philippians 3:20, 21; I Thessalonians 1:9, 10; I Thessalonians 4:13-18; I John 3:2, 3

This "blessed hope" of believers in Christ is often called the rapture, or translation, of the Church. It is the next event, we believe, in God's revealed program.

9. What does this promise mean to sorrowing saints?

I Thessalonians 4:18 _____

10. What bearing does it have upon the practical Christian life?

I John 2:28; 3:2, 3 _____

_____

11. What will take place in connection with Jesus' coming for His Church?

I Thessalonians 4:16, 17 _____

12. Why will one company of Christians never have to pass through death?

I Corinthians 15:51, 52 _____

_____

The "great tribulation"

13. After the rapture of the Church, what will immediately precede Christ's coming in power?

Matthew 24:21, 29 _____

14. How will the peoples of the earth be affected?

Matthew 24:30 _____

"The glorious appearing of . . . Jesus Christ" (TITUS 2:13)

15. How will the Lord Jesus come the second time?

MATTHEW 16:27; 24:30 _____

16. When He comes to reign, how will He be manifested to the world?

MATTHEW 24:27 _____

17. What did Jesus say about the time of His second coming?

MATTHEW 24:36; ACTS 1:7 _____

18. Will the world be converted before His second coming?

MATTHEW 24:38, 39 _____

19. Since no one knows the time of His coming, what exhortation did Jesus leave to His people?

MATTHEW 24:42; 25:13 _____

20. What hint did Jesus give His disciples as to the length of time it might be before He returned?

MATTHEW 25:19 _____

21. When He returns in power and glory, what will He do?

MATTHEW 25:31, 32 _____

22. What did Jesus say of those who are ashamed of Him in this life?

MARK 8:38 _____

23. What should be the continual attitude of Christians, in view of the promise of Jesus' return?

Luke 12:35-37 _____

_____

24. What was Jesus' parting message to the Jews who rejected Him?

Luke 13:35 _____

25. What warning did Jesus give concerning false claims that He had arrived quietly on earth?

Matthew 24:25-27; Luke 17:23, 24 _____

26. What question did Jesus raise as to general religious conditions in the days just preceding His return?

Luke 18:8 _____

_____

27. What did He indicate as to world conditions?

Luke 21:26 _____

_____

28. According to the Lord Jesus, who will deceive many prior to His return?

Matthew 24:11 _____

29. What was the angelic message, given as Jesus ascended into heaven?

Acts 1:10, 11 _____

_____

30. According to Scripture, will His coming be literal and personal or spiritual, such as the progress of knowledge and social justice?

Acts 1:11; I Thessalonians 4:15, 16; Revelation 1:7 _____

_____

God's purpose for this Church age

31. What is the divine purpose for this age, ending when Jesus returns?

a. Acts 15:14 _____

b. Romans 11:25 _____

32. Did Jesus commission believers to convert the entire world?

Matthew 24:14 _____

33. What did He give as His program for the Church?

Matthew 28:19 _____

34. Was there any intimation that all men would at any time be converted as a result of this preaching?

Mark 16:15 _____

We do not deny the power of the gospel to accomplish its full design; but we hold that the Scriptures teach that the gospel was not designed to convert the whole world in this age, but rather to call out "a people for his name" (Acts 15:14).

Signs of the end of the age

What is the difference between premillennialism and postmillennialism?

Premillennialists believe the Bible teaches that Christ is to return at the close of the present evil age; and that He Himself, with His accompanying angelic hosts, will separate the good from the bad, after which He will personally reign as King throughout the millennial age.

Postmillennialists believe that all things are, during the present age, moving irresistibly forward toward the golden age; that man himself will, through religious teaching and the advances of science and education, succeed in purging the earth and setting up the millennial kingdom; and that Christ will not return until the close of this perfect age. (The perilous times that have followed two world wars must cause disillusionment among many!)

35. What is given as one sign of the coming of the Lord?

I Thessalonians 5:3 _____

_____

36. Will enlightened believers be deceived about the talk of world peace?

I Thessalonians 5:4 _____

37. What is prophesied concerning conditions near the end of this Church age?

II Thessalonians 2:3 _____

_____

38. To what extremes will some go in their departure from the faith, as the age draws to a close?

I Timothy 4:1 _____

_____

39. What will this lead them to do?

I Timothy 4:2, 3 _____

_____

40. Will the last days be safe times?

II Timothy 3:1 _____

41. How will sin be manifest?

II Timothy 3:2-4 _____

_____

42. What will characterize apostate churches?

II Timothy 3:5 _____

43. What condition will prevail?

II Timothy 3:7 _____

44. While parts of the world may improve materially, with inventions and conveniences, what will be its condition morally?

II TIMOTHY 3:13 _____

45. Will gospel preaching be popular in the last days?

II TIMOTHY 4:3, 4 _____

_____

46. What condition will exist as to increased wealth on the part of some?

JAMES 5:1-6 _____

_____

47. What should the attitude of Christians be under these conditions?

JAMES 5:7, 8 _____

_____

48. Who will increase before Christ comes?

II PETER 2:1 _____

49. Will false teaching prevail?

II PETER 2:2 _____

_____

50. What attitude will many religious leaders take toward the truth of the Lord's coming?

II PETER 3:3, 4 _____

_____

51. Will their denials change the truth?

II PETER 3:9, 10 _____

check-up time No. 8

You have just studied some important truths about Christ's second advent. Review your study by re-reading the questions and your written answers. If you aren't sure of an answer, reread the Scripture portion given to see if you can find the answer. Then take this test to see how well you understand important truths you have studied.

In the right-hand margin write "True" or "False" after each of the following statements.

1. All the world will be converted before the coming of Christ. _____

2. False prophets will increase before the coming of Christ. _____

3. Only God knows the day of the return of Christ. _____

4. The believers who have died will be raised when Christ returns. _____

5. Moral conditions on earth will get better before Christ's return. _____

6. Many will scoff at the truth of the Lord's return. _____

7. Prior to the return of Christ, religion will have a form of godliness, but little power. _____

8. Christ's program for the Church until He returns is to preach the gospel. _____

9. The return of Christ will be literal and personal. _____

10. Christians are to watch diligently and wait for Christ's coming. _____

Turn to page 80 and check your answers.

The Person and Work of the Holy Spirit

Bible Teaching About the Holy Spirit

The Holy Spirit—a Person in the Godhead

We should refer to the Holy Spirit, the third Person of the Trinity, as a divine personality, possessing individual substance, intelligence and will; we must not refer to Him as "it." His personality appears from His attributes and works.

1. How many times do we find the personal pronoun used of the Holy Spirit in JOHN 14—16?

_____

2. According to GENESIS 1:2, in what work did He have part?

_____

3. What does the book of Job say?

JOB 33:4 _____

4. In what work of God did the Spirit have a part?

PSALM 104:30 _____

5. What does He do in relation to men?

GENESIS 6:3 _____

6. What is He able to do for the physical man?

JUDGES 14:6, 19 _____

7. Who gives the believer wisdom and ability for leadership? JUDGES 3:10 _____

8. According to PSALM 139:7, what divine attribute has the Holy Spirit?

_____

9. Through whose agency are sinners born into God's kingdom? JOHN 3:5-8; TITUS 3:5, 6 _____

10. What did Jesus say about the ministry of the Spirit?

JOHN 14:16, 17 _____

_____

11. Why was the Holy Spirit's descent at Pentecost essential to the disciples and the rapid spread of the gospel?

LUKE 24:49; ACTS 1:8 _____

12. What miraculous signs accompanied the Spirit's coming at Pentecost, to demonstrate fully that Jesus had kept His promise to send "another Comforter"?

ACTS 2:1-4 _____

13. In this Church age, what is the permanent relationship between the Holy Spirit and the believer?

ROMANS 8:9 _____

_____

14. What does the experience of spiritual birth make of the believer's body?

I CORINTHIANS 6:19 _____

_____

15. What is the condition of receiving the Holy Spirit?

JOHN 7:37-39 _____

_____

16. When one truly believes on Jesus Christ as his personal Saviour, what does the Holy Spirit do for him?

EPHESIANS 1:13, 14 _____

17. This seal of the Spirit is a pledge of what day?

EPHESIANS 1:14; 4:30; ROMANS 8:23 _____

The convicting work of the Spirit

18. What special work does the Holy Spirit do?

JOHN 16:8-11 _____

19. What is said of the natural man?

I CORINTHIANS 2:14 _____

_____

20. Who makes the Bible become to the Christian a Book filled with treasures?

I CORINTHIANS 2:9-16 _____

Wherever there is a praying heart, the Holy Spirit waits to convert the soul and make God's Word become "quick [or, living] and powerful" (HEBREWS 4:12).

21. Can anyone truly acknowledge Jesus as Lord and Saviour apart from the Holy Spirit's work in the heart?

I CORINTHIANS 12:3 _____

Christ is "the door" into God's presence (JOHN 10:9). Faith is the key that unlocks the door (ROMANS 10:17). The Holy Spirit gives one the key and helps him turn it in the lock for access (EPHESIANS 2:18).

22. What warning is given concerning the way one should receive the Holy Spirit, when He comes knocking at the door of the heart?

_____

The work of the Spirit in the believer

23. After one has been born of the Spirit, what exhortation applies to him?

EPHESIANS 5:18; ACTS 6:3 _____

_____

24. Having recevied the Spirit through union with Christ, how does one receive the fullness of the Spirit for service?

ROMANS 6:13, 16 _____

25. How may we have fullness of power for service?

JOHN 7:37-39 _____

"Drink" suggests appropriation—faith in Christ for every need.

26. Against what is the Christian warned, lest he should lose the sense of the Spirit's blessing?

a. EPHESIANS 4:30 _____

b. I THESSALONIANS 5:19 _____

We grieve the Spirit by permitting in our lives the things which we know are contrary to God's will. We quench Him by resisting His energy and work in us and by refusing to do as He prompts us (I CORINTHIANS 12:8-11; ACTS 13:2-4; 16:6, 7; 8:29).

27. What is the outward test of one's claim to the indwelling and filling by the Holy Spirit?

GALATIANS 5:22, 23 _____

_____

check-up time No. 9

You have just studied some important truths about the Person and work of the Holy Spirit. Review your study by rereading the questions and your written answers. If you aren't sure of an answer, reread the Scripture portion given to see if you can find the answer. Then take this test to see how well you understand important truths you have studied.

In the right-hand margin write "True" or "False" after each of the following statements.

1. One can acknowledge Jesus as Lord and Saviour apart from the Spirit's work in his heart. _____

2. The natural man understands the things of the Spirit of God. _____

3. The Spirit seals the believer until the day of redemption. _____

4. It is the work of the Spirit to convict the world of sin. _____

5. The Scriptures teach that the Holy Spirit had a part in the creation of the world. _____

6. The believer is filled with the Spirit by yielding himself wholly to God. _____

7. The believer's body is the temple of the Holy Spirit. _____

8. The fruit of the Spirit is the outward test of one's claim to the indwelling and filling by the Spirit. _____

9. Grieving the Spirit will cause the believer to lose the sense of the Spirit's blessing. _____

10. The Spirit indwells the believer. _____

Turn to page 80 and check your answers.

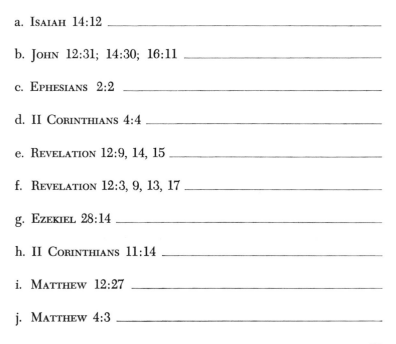

Bible Doctrine of Satan

The reality of a personal devil

The Bible teaching about the devil is unwelcome to many; yet the Scriptures everywhere teach the existence of a personal spirit of evil. Moreover, the facts of human life attest the existence of a superior diabolical spirit who works upon the fallen nature of man, suggesting evil.

Our Lord met a personal devil in the wilderness (MATTHEW 4:1-11).

Personal names are ascribed to the devil. He is called *Satan* thirty-five times in the New Testament.

1. What is he called in the following passages?

a. ISAIAH 14:12 _____

b. JOHN 12:31; 14:30; 16:11 _____

c. EPHESIANS 2:2 _____

d. II CORINTHIANS 4:4 _____

e. REVELATION 12:9, 14, 15 _____

f. REVELATION 12:3, 9, 13, 17 _____

g. EZEKIEL 28:14 _____

h. II CORINTHIANS 11:14 _____

i. MATTHEW 12:27 _____

j. MATTHEW 4:3 _____

59

k. I PETER 5:8 _____

l. I JOHN 2:13; 3:12; 5:18 _____

m. II CORINTHIANS 6:15 _____

n. JOHN 8:44 _____

o. REVELATION 12:10 _____

2. Is the work of Satan distinguished from the work of the flesh and the world?

EPHESIANS 2:2, 3; JAMES 4:4; I JOHN 2:3, 4 _____

The fall of Lucifer

3. What do you learn in EZEKIEL 28:11-19 about Satan's origin?

_____

_____

4. About the cause of his fall?

_____

_____

5. About his future outlook?

_____

_____

6. What does ISAIAH 14:12-15 say about the reason for his downfall?

_____

_____

7. About his ultimate fate?

_____

_____

Two significant events of Satan's history are (a) his triumph over the first Adam; (b) his defeat at the hands of the last Adam.

8. In what three ways did Satan tempt Eve?

GENESIS 3; compare I JOHN 2:16 _____

_____

_____

9. a. How did the enemy appeal to "the lust of the flesh"?

_____

b. "The lust of the eye"?

_____

c. "The pride of life"?

_____

10. Did Satan make similar appeals to Christ in the wilderness?

MATTHEW 4:1-11 _____

The evil nature of Satan

11. How is the devil described in the following passages?

a. PSALM 91:3 _____

b. II TIMOTHY 2:26 _____

c. MATTHEW 13:39 _____

d. LUKE 22:31-34 _____

e. MATTHEW 24:24; II CORINTHIANS 11:14 _____

f. II CORINTHIANS 12:7-10 _____

g. EPHESIANS 6:12, 13 _____

Why did God permit sin in the world?

Men have argued to no avail over the question of why God created Lucifer, knowing that he would fall, and why He permitted him to introduce sin into the world. The fact is that sin is here. It has invaded human society.

The Genesis account is a vindication of God. He created man innocent and happy, giving him delightful surroundings and a "helpmeet," or companion. Desiring from him the trustful obedience of a child—not the enforced obedience of a slave—God gave him the power of choice, with full warning of the consequence of disobedience.

Since man was created with the capacity of choice and moral perception of a high order, his environment had to include provision for the use of these powers. Hence Satan was permitted to enter the scene and test man.

All the unregenerate are wholly on Satan's territory

12. In the following passages what are the unsaved called?

a. MATTHEW 13:38 _____

b. JOHN 8:44 _____

c. ACTS 13:10 _____

d. EPHESIANS 2:2; COLOSSIANS 3:6 _____

e. EPHESIANS 2:3 _____

13. What relation does Satan have to all who are lost?

EPHESIANS 2:1, 2 _____

_____

Christians should resist the devil

14. In view of Satan's ability to suggest evil, what are believers exhorted to do?

a. I PETER 5:8 _____

b. EPHESIANS 4:27 _____

c. JAMES 4:7; I PETER 5:9 _____

d. EPHESIANS 6:11 _____

15. With what weapon?

EPHESIANS 6:17 _____

16. What did Jesus do?

MATTHEW 17:18 _____

17. Why does no believer need to be defeated by the devil?

I JOHN 4:4 _____

18. How are those, referred to in REVELATION 12:11, said to over-come Satan?

REVELATION 12:11 _____

The doom of Satan

19. What is prepared for the devil?

MATTHEW 25:41 _____

_____

20. What will be done to him when Jesus returns to reign?

REVELATION 20:1-3 _____

21. What will take place after the thousand year reign?

REVELATION 20:7-9 _____

22. What will be Satan's final doom?

REVELATION 20:10 _____

23. What will become of all his works?

I JOHN 3:8 _____

24. What death blow has already been delivered to Satan's dominion?

JOHN 12:31 _____

25. How is the believer delivered from the fear of death?

HEBREWS 2:14, 15 _____

_____

You have just studied some important truths about the Bible doctrine of Satan. Review your study by rereading the questions and your written answers. If you aren't sure of an answer, reread the Scripture portion given to see if you can find the answer. Then take this test to see how well you understand important truths you have studied.

In the right-hand margin write "True" or "False" after each of the following statements.

1. Believers can't help being defeated by the devil because he is stronger than they. _____

2. The death of Christ delivers the believer from the fear of death. _____

3. The Word of God is the believer's weapon against Satan. _____

4. Christ will cast Satan into the bottomless pit, from which, with great cunning, he will escape. _____

5. The unsaved are called children of the devil. _____

6. Satan fell from his original state because of pride. _____

7. Satan is described as an angel of darkness. _____

8. Satan was a beautiful thing in his original creation. _____

9. The believer should resist the devil. _____

10. Satan will ultimately be victorious over Christ. _____

Turn to page 80 and check your answers.

Basic Principles of the Gospel

"Ye must be born again" (JOHN 3:7)

The fundamental basis of the gospel is that men are lost without Jesus Christ; and that apart from acceptance of His vicarious sacrifice, they cannot reach heaven.

1. Since this is the case, lost men must be regenerated—born from above. That which is born of the flesh is flesh; therefore, ye

_____. JOHN 3:6, 7

2. What is our state by nature as we enter this world?

PSALM 51:5 _____

3. How soon do we begin to go astray?

PSALM 58:3 _____

4. What is the real condition of the unregenerate heart?

JEREMIAH 17:9 _____

5. Of what are all guilty?

ROMANS 3:23 _____

6. By nature we are _____. EPHESIANS 2:1

Christ is "the way . . ." (JOHN 14:6)

7. To be saved, what must one have implanted in him?

II PETER 1:4 _____

8. As soon as one has life through Christ, he is made

_____. II CORINTHIANS 5:17

9. Through acceptance of Him _____

_____. EPHESIANS 2:5; COLOSSIANS 2:13

10. What is the one way of salvation, as revealed in the Bible?

JOHN 14:6 _____

11. Through what name alone does God give salvation?

ACTS 4:12 _____

12. Who has offered the one and only atonement for sin?

HEBREWS 9:22, 28 _____

13. Who alone has saving power?

I JOHN 5:12; JOHN 6:44 _____

14. What does the Bible say of one who preaches some other way of salvation?

GALATIANS 1:8, 9 _____

_____

"Faith cometh by hearing . . . the word of God" (ROMANS 10:17)

Where the gospel is believed, missions and evangelism are certain to follow. Since there is no salvation apart from Jesus Christ, the gospel must be given to those who are to be saved.

15. How does the apostle Paul stress the necessity of evangelism?

ROMANS 10:14, 15 _____

_____

16. Write out our Lord's Great Commission.

MATTHEW 28:19, 20 _____

_____

_____

_____

17. What is the instrument through which men are born of God?

a. JAMES 1:18 _____

b. I PETER 1:23 _____

18. Faith cometh by _____. ROMANS 10:17

All are "without excuse" before God (ROMANS 1:18-20)

19. Do those who have never heard of the written Word, already have a law to which God can justly hold them accountable?

ROMANS 2:14, 15 _____

20. How is it possible for the heathen to know whether or not there is a God before they have heard the gospel?

ROMANS 1:20 _____

_____

21. What witness does every man born into the world have?

PSALM 19:1, 4 _____

22. Is sincere belief in some heathen religion accepted of God as a basis of salvation?

ISAIAH 9:16, 17; PROVERBS 16:25 _____

_____

Many missionaries have testified to finding in heathen lands those who had been sincerely groping after the true God, and who looked upon the missionary's arrival as the answer to their prayers. For the most part, however, the heathen do not walk in the light they already have, but choose rather the pleasures of sin; hence they may be justly held accountable. They are lost because they are deliberately living contrary to the light of conscience and nature which they already have. This does not mean that future retribution is the same for all, for this is to be graded according to works and according to the light against which one has sinned.

"Ye shall be witnesses unto me" (ACTS 1:8)

All believers should be missionaries. Remember that the Bible does not divide the world into home and foreign misisonary fields. It divides the human race into just two classes—saved and lost—and places upon the saved the responsibility of telling the unsaved of Christ's redeeming power.

23. What does the Lord Jesus want every Christian to be?

MATTHEW 4:19 _____

24. What title does Paul give the Christians?

II CORINTHIANS 5:20 _____

25. What responsibility does the Lord Jesus place upon every believer?

MATTHEW 5:13-16 _____

_____

26. What should Christians be in their daily lives?

II CORINTHIANS 3:3 _____

27. What is defined as an essential accompaniment of salvation?

ROMANS 10:9, 10 _____

28. "Out of the abundance of _____

_____." LUKE 6:45

29. Why is it that many professing Christians do not bear witness to Christ?

PROVERBS 29:25 _____

30. If a Christian wants God's guidance in his own life, what should he do?

PROVERBS 3:6 _____

31. If one has experienced the power of redemption, what does he owe to Christ?

PSALM 107:2 _____

32. What does Jesus promise to do for those who bear witness for Him?

MATTHEW 10:32, 33 _____

33. What does He say of those who are ashamed of Him before men?

MARK 8:38 _____

34. What should all followers of Christ be able to say?

ROMANS 1:16 _____

_____

_____

Not only is confessing Christ to others a necessity from the standpoint of instruction to the lost, but it is an essential means of spiritual development for the Christian. The more we assert and declare a truth, the stronger its hold upon us. It increases and develops faith and deepens our love for Christ (I JOHN 4:15, 16).

check-up time No. 11

You have just studied some important truths about the basic principles of the gospel. Review your study by rereading the questions and your written answers. If you aren't sure of an answer, reread the Scripture portion given to see if you can find the answer. Then take this test to see how well you understand important truths you have studied.

In the right-hand margin write "True" or "False" after each of the following statements.

1. The Word of God has a part in bringing salvation to mankind. _____

2. Jesus wants every Christian to be a fisher of men. _____

3. It is possible for the heathen to know whether or not there is a God before they have heard the gospel. _____

4. We are sinless when we enter the world at birth. _____

5. As soon as one has life through Christ, he is made a new creature. _____

6. Christ has offered the one and only atonement for sin. _____

7. Sincere belief in some heathen religion is accepted of God as a basis of salvation. _____

8. Many professing Christians fail to witness because they are afraid of the criticism of men. _____

9. The Scripture pronounces a curse on all who preach any other way of salvation. _____

10. All followers of Christ should be able to say that they are not ashamed of the gospel. _____

Turn to page 80 and check your answers.

Vital Truths of the Faith

Grace

1. What clear distinction does the New Testament make as stated, for example, in JOHN 1:17?

_____

_____

2. Could the works of the law save anyone?

GALATIANS 3:21, 22 _____

3. What purpose does the law serve?

ROMANS 3:19 _____

_____

4. Why can't the law save anyone?

ROMANS 8:3, 4 _____

_____

5. How can sinful men be saved?

a. EPHESIANS 2:8, 9 _____

b. TITUS 3:5, 6 _____

_____

6. Can salvation be partly of grace (unmerited favor) and partly of works?

ROMANS 11:6; GALATIANS 3:18 _____

Faith

The basic idea of faith is that of committing oneself to the promises of God's Word.

7. Faith is believing _____. ACTS 27:25

8. What is always the blessed result of taking God at His Word?

LUKE 1:45 _____

9. Faith is the assurance that _____

_____. ROMANS 4:21

10. What two elements enter into faith?

HEBREWS 11:6 _____

_____

11. What are the effects of faith as described in HEBREWS 11:1?

_____

12. What is the basis of faith?

ROMANS 10:17 _____

13. What is the first result of faith in God's Word?

JOHN 1:12 _____

14. How may a Christian have his faith deepened?

LUKE 17:5 _____

15. How is faith imparted to one?

I CORINTHIANS 12:8, 9 _____

Justification

Justification is the act of God whereby He declares one righteous who believes in Jesus Christ as his personal Saviour.

16. Is there any possibility of one's being justified before God through his own works?

LUKE 10:29; 16:15; ROMANS 9:31, 32 _____

17. What is the emphatic statement of the apostle Paul?

GALATIANS 2:16 _____

_____

18. What is the only possible basis for having this standing before God?

ROMANS 3:28 _____

_____

19. What is the ground of justification?

ROMANS 3:24; TITUS 3:7 _____

20. Through whose work alone is justification made possible?

ROMANS 4:5 _____

21. How did He procure this justification?

ROMAN 5:9 _____

22. What else enters into our justification?

ROMANS 4:25 _____

23. What will be the first effect in the believer's life of appropriating the finished work of Christ?

ROMANS 5:1 _____

24. What is the proof of justification by faith?

JAMES 2:24 _____

_____

Assurance

25. When one has divine righteousness set to his account, what should be the natural effects?

Isaiah 32:17 _____

_____

Assurance is the full confidence, possessed by a believer, that he has salvation, in which he will be forever kept by the power of God.

26. With what is the experience of assurance linked?

Hebrews 10:22 _____

27. How did Paul express his assurance?

II Timothy 1:12 _____

_____

_____

28. What reason for assurance did Jesus give the believer?

John 10:28, 29 _____

_____

_____

29. Since Christ represents us in heaven, can any charge against us stand?

Romans 8:33, 34 _____

30. If a Christian sins, is there any ground of assurance left for him?

I John 2:1, 2 _____

31. What work of the Holy Spirit furnishes further ground of assurance?

EPHESIANS 1:13, 14 _____

32. With what is this sense of assurance linked?

HEBREWS 6:11, 12 _____

33. Upon what must assurance always be grounded?

I JOHN 5:13 _____

34. What is sure to accompany a genuine assurance?

I JOHN 3:14 _____

Salvation is offered to the unsaved as a free gift (ROMANS 6:23).

Rewards

Rewards are held before believers as an incentive to faithful service.

35. What did Jesus say about the most humble service rendered for His sake?

MATTHEW 10:42 _____

36. How did He say that faith would be honored in the coming day?

LUKE 19:17 _____

37. What will Christ do about believers' works when He comes for His own?

I CORINTHIANS 3:11, 14; REVELATION 22:12 _____

38. To win rewards, what must we do?

I CORINTHIANS 3:8 _____

39. Can anyone labor for salvation?

JOHN 6:28, 29 _____

_____

40. Though we may receive little recognition from men for our service, of what may we be certain?

MATTHEW 16:27; 25:19; I PETER 5:4 _____

41. For what will a special crown be given?

JAMES 1:12 _____

42. For what service is a great reward promised?

DANIEL 12:3 _____

43. On what foundation must these works be built in order for the believer to receive a reward?

I CORINTHIANS 3:11-15 _____

_____

44. At the judgment seat of Christ, will our works be tested primarily as to their quantity or their quality?

I CORINTHIANS 3:13; II CORINTHIANS 5:10 _____

45. If, in that day, Christian's works are not of enduring character, according to I CORINTHIANS 3:15,

a. What will he lose? _____

b. What will he have left? _____

You have just studied some important Bible teaching about vital truths of the Christian faith. Review your study by rereading the questions and your written answers. If you aren't sure of an answer, reread the Scripture portion given to see if you can find the answer. Then take this test to see how well you understand important truths you have studied.

In the right-hand margin write "True" or "False" after each of the following statements.

1. Only spectacular service for God will be rewarded. _____

2. Justification comes through good works. _____

3. The believer will be tested for the quantity of his works. _____

4. Salvation is partly of grace and partly of works. _____

5. Faith is the assurance that what God has promised He is able to perform. _____

6. All rewards for the Christian will be realized during his lifetime on earth. _____

7. The function of the law is to make people aware of personal sin. _____

8. The believer has assurance because he is kept in the hands of the Father and the Son. _____

9. At the judgment seat of Christ, the believer will receive no reward for works which are not of enduring character. _____

10. The one who feels he needs faith can work it up within himself. _____

Turn to page 80 and check your answers.

Suggestions for class use

1. The class teacher may wish to tear this page from each workbook as the answer key is on the reverse side.

2. The teacher should study the lesson first, filling in the blanks in the workbook. He should be prepared to give help to the class on some of the harder places in the lesson. He should also take the self-check tests himself, check his answers with the answer key and look up any question answered incorrectly.

3. Class sessions can be supplemented by the teacher's giving a talk or leading a discussion on the subject to be studied. The class could then fill in the workbook together as a group, in teams, or individually. If so desired by the teacher, however, this could be done at home. The self-check tests can be done as homework by the class.

4. The self-check tests can be corrected at the beginning of each class session. A brief discussion of the answers can serve as review for the previous lesson.

5. The teacher should motivate and encourage his students. Some public recognition might well be given to class members who successfully complete this course.

Moody Press, a ministry of the Moody Bible Institute, is designed for education, evangelization and edification. If we may assist you in knowing more about Christ and the Christian life, please write us without obligation to:
Moody Press, c/o MLM, Chicago, Illinois 60610.

answer key
to self-check tests

Be sure to look up any questions you answered incorrectly.

A gives the correct *answer*.

R *refers* you back to the number of the question in the lesson itself, where the correct answer is to be found.

Mark with an "x" your wrong answers.

Question	TEST 1 A	TEST 1 R	TEST 2 A	TEST 2 R	TEST 3 A	TEST 3 R	TEST 4 A	TEST 4 R	TEST 5 A	TEST 5 R	TEST 6 A	TEST 6 R
1	T	14	F	10	T	21	F	2	T	45	T	2
2	F	12	F	3	T	17	T	8	F	31	F	22
3	F	3	T	7	T	33	T	14	T	40	T	13
4	F	13	F	4	T	2	T	33	T	38	T	5
5	T	12	T	14	T	26	F	3	F	22	T	7
6	T	4	T	5	T	18	T	24	T	5	T	29
7	T	18	T	8	T	28	F	22	F	50	F	17
8	F	6	T	9	F	10	T	27	T	7	T	8
9	T	1	F	18	T	35	T	9	T	33	T	6
10	F	6	T	6	T	25	T	20	T	19	F	23

Question	TEST 7 A	TEST 7 R	TEST 8 A	TEST 8 R	TEST 9 A	TEST 9 R	TEST 10 A	TEST 10 R	TEST 11 A	TEST 11 R	TEST 12 A	TEST 12 R
1	T	21	F	18	F	21	F	17	T	18	F	35
2	T	4	T	28	F	19	T	25	T	23	F	17
3	T	2	T	17	T	17	T	15	T	20	F	44
4	F	18	T	11	T	18	F	21	F	2	F	6
5	T	23	F	41	T	2	T	12	T	8	T	9
6	T	1	T	50	T	24	T	4	T	12	F	37
7	T	9	T	42	T	14	F	11	F	22	T	3
8	T	14	T	33	T	27	T	3	T	29	T	28
9	F	8	T	30	T	26	T	14	T	14	T	45
10	T	13	T	23	T	13	F	22	T	34	F	15

how well did you do?

0-1 wrong answers—excellent work

2-3 wrong answers—review errors carefully

4 or more wrong answers—restudy the lesson before going on to the next one